THE B........LIBRARY

THE BONE LIBRARY

Jenni Fagan

First published in paperback in Great Britain in 2022 by
Polygon, an imprint of Birlinn Ltd.

Birlinn Ltd
West Newington House
10 Newington Road
Edinburgh
EH9 1QS

9 8 7 6 5 4 3 2 1

www.polygonbooks.co.uk

ISBN 978 1 84697 592 9
eBook ISBN 978 1 78885 521 1

British Library Cataloguing-in-Publication Data
A catalogue record for this book is available
from the British Library.

The publisher gratefully acknowledges investment from
Creative Scotland towards the publication of this book.

Typeset in Verdigris M V B by Polygon, Edinburgh
Printed and bound in Great Britain by CPI Group (UK)
Ltd, Croydon CR0 4YY

CONTENTS

I'M NOT A FOSSIL, YOU ARE A CURIO

My darling ossein, I have known your organic extracellular matrix
since the first seconds it began to form, still . . .

Your bones did not come from my bones,
they coalesced in ether

where all osteoblasts dawn,
tell me . . . how many carcasses are walking this earth?

The utter idiocy of vessels!
Some poor skeletons have such twisted minds to carry.

Ones who must think this – is all there is?
Delusions tell them they shan't be judged on their actions,

in a place that will make this one look
pallid on the petrochemical

motions of Minerva,
such inciters of insanity and loss . . .

My dear sweet toxic male gene,
what's your fucking issue with humanity?

I raise one of yours and he is fuck all
like so very many of you,

this generation are better than those
before and their bones did not come from our bones,

they arose from the dust of dinosaurs
imbued with glacier hearts,

blazed their way into existence,
in the unlikeliest of flesh forms,

what a confine! Thing is,
you were the only one who ever taught me

the meaning of love,
you are the firn in all its truth.

I am genuinely sorry my life has been so strange as this,
it's a burden, I know it . . .

But the joy, the absolute utter brilliance
in just knowing – you, good day/bad, mercurial/sad,

raging/peaceful . . . trying,
in all of it, your bones taught my bones how to walk.

Your bones . . . taught . . . my bones, how to walk!
I am so grateful and this world . . .

It owes you and so do I,
so much more

than this, so I will lay my bones
down on the road –

just one more time, for you,
I'd do it ten more, ten thousand,

I'll do whatever I can, so you, can one day,
for a second,

be safe awhile in your home,
sit on an old porch

and maybe sometimes
take a moment to remember

the woman you came from . . .
who was humble enough and smart enough to know,

your bones belong to no one,
you came into this life owned

by no false gods,
it's a strange story that tells us otherwise . . .

I'll defend whatever I can –
of your autonomy,

my child, I love every single bone in you,
bow to nobody, be free.

THE NINETEEN THIRTIES HOUSE

I keep putting slugs
out the cat flap
at night,

and nobody loves me
and children
are dying.

Slug trails silver tiles
tiny moons
hang from boughs

an iridescent tree,
across my kitchen floor
each morning,

and one person
does actually
love me

but nobody
holds me
and each day I die,

I do it
so much better
than that old wanker –

his burned retinas
haloed in twelve
worlds –

I'm a prick
really and my dying
is sadly ineffective

my loneliness no
more pathetic
than yours, Poncho

and yes, the children
need me to be
marching

and there are so many people
who must hear us
scream – no?

Instead, they pour gold
into their auricles –
excision

of empathy
is required
to dine

on the souls
of those without . . .
and there are so

many slugs
on my kitchen
floor,

and I keep
picking them up on a spoon,
placing them carefully

out the cat flap
and the world . . .
she wants her rivers back

sent helix & virus
to claim them
and it's only the start

of her human invasion,
can't tame her
whilst all I dumbly want,

is the right kind of someone
to hold me,
but it seems as likely

as this world
held hostage by fucking mentalists
sorting out its shit.

WHO ARE YOU?

Who are you?
In the kitchen window. Grinding coffee. Counting birds of mourning.

Who are you?
Too shallow bath. Black hair wet and plastered to your body.

Who are you?
Selector of films. The one who called and asked what I thought.

Who are you?
Footsteps on the stair, annoyed by my heart's loud beat, so it beats.

Who are you?
Inside my body. Not inside my body. Not interested. Interested.

Who are you?
Happy to see me. It feels rare. Rare loss. Thinks I have no point ever.
    An incubator of madness.

Who are you?
Wrapping twine around my memories and saying they are heather.

Who are you?
Teller of stories of better places. Teller of who I am. Teller of brown eyes.

Who are you?
Taller when unreadable, and taller when you want to be.

Who are you?
Leaving with a packed bag for eternity. Eternity has no station. I should
     have told you.

Who are you?
Back. Again, holding a hand-out, dry knuckled reader.

Who are you?
The person I hear in all the minutes and at waking and when the owls
     are asleep.

Who are you?
In a cinema, eyelids closed whilst the shining shines. You'd sleep
     forever to avoid mine.

Who are you?
Cat between us most nights, to her you like.

Who are you?
Keeper of no time in the shadows.

Who are you?
How am I meant to know? If you do not look me in the eye in bed. If
     you do not know yourself?

Who are you?
When the tears end? When silence has been shorn. When you no longer
     nod to me in my own hall.

ON THE FILES

It says nobody knows
where I lived
for the first three months
of my life –

I say, goblins:
poet ones who smoked cigarettes
and had great taste
in foundlings.

THE BONE LIBRARY

I arrived in The Bone Library
minus my heart –
isn't it always the way?

I needed heart mitosis,
a transplant.
I had two hundred and six human bones:

chromatic DNA
bones filed –
no click-clack

vertebrate.
There were a great many secrets
filed in The Bone Library.

Drawers with skull,
jaw, spine, cervical, thoracic, lumbar
sacrum and tailbone,

chest, scapula, clavicle,
humerus, radius, ulna,
ribs and breastbone.

I was in bits
when I arrived here!
I was in so many parts

you could roll me out in sections,
glide me back in again –
tiny wrist bones (carpals)

metacarpals and phalanges,
hip bones
lay wide open

like a mermaid's welcome,
two smooth thigh bones
(femur): sounds

kind of feline;
kneecaps (patella);
shin bone (tibia); fibula

all before feet –
with their tarsals and metatarsals,
sweet refrain of phalanges,

Osteocytes.
Osteoclasts.
Osteolight.

I met a man with bones for teeth
and he bared 'em like a whale
in the great blue deep.

There should be a piano . . .
in The Bone Library,
with long bones

for keys,
short bones painted black for high notes,
smooth flat bones

for laying a cup of tea (or wine)
(or gin) (or love note),
please do, send one to me –

there is an irregular bone in every one of us
it's not for conforming,
merci, merci, merci!

THE TRUTH IS OLD AND IT WANTS TO GO HOME

One of the ten mothers
(not the worst one but still a steady killer)
would never let me grow my hair at all;
it had to be short
like a boy.
There was a zero-tolerance policy
to me ever remotely
thinking
I could be considered nice, or likeable, or pretty.

When I was five, she'd hide her purse.
Me being a thief was a graveyard type concern, long before she met me.
She told me I'd go to prison.
One day.
One day!
Any day now . . .
Soon!
It starts with ten pence for a penny mixture you see, and then before
     you know it . . .
you're banged up and doing life.

I'd have to get old enough for that of course,
get stabilizers off my bike
maybe learn to write a bit better,
what I had to learn first and most solemnly and sincerely and viciously
     though,
was that I – was not a thing to be trusted, no!
She wrote me a letter when I was seven or eight,
stating that if (when?) I grew up to be a murderer,
or a lesbian, or get HIV, she would still love me.
Hopeful she seemed. That's what I might grow up to be.

SUMMERHALL ALMANAC

Artists fade among us –
at twilight they carve tiny animations,

endless precision
to pour truth, triumph, trauma

into image,
just to touch a heart . . .

so it might shatter
or ameliorate –

they paint this world
out of sheer choler.

Injustice
is a paintbrush

daubed in the dishonour of nations
take the structures down!

Artists fight each other whilst
brazing truth in zinc,

hammer it into stone,
set it on fire,

lay it under the moon,
they reimagine

what might make up humanity,
in amaranthine rooms

they pick up instruments,
play until fingertips bleed,

tune up to their own heart's beat,
it's only a metronome,

write until they lose affiliation
to normalcy –

forget it and sunlight –
whittle poems

into arrows
to strike a stranger's soul,

lest it has not been pierced so well lately –
exalt your strange

in all its fragile –
extraordinary,

and when,
with considerable sadness,

they remove
every single last star

from the sky,
it is only so the absence of light

will let you dream
with greater luminescence,

and they know all things only become truly unique
or beautiful

when shattered, then they can become whole,
fill each crack with gold,

inappropriately excessive in their desire to reach,
erratically hopeful.

If you meet one,
I ask one thing,

please be fucking kind,
it's hard

to make art
out of the darkness

and bind it,
with your own soul's light.

THE GOOD STUFF

The good stuff
(is rare)
but if you find
it you will
know
it in all your levels –
the best art
restarts the atriums,
invisible, it works on the body,
shocks it if necessary,
however many volts it takes,
to start your life again,
in that moment,
like open-heart
surgery.

I KNOW WHO I AM

I know who I am
although others often make me forget,

with their pelican hunger.
The pistons in my mind alarm them!

I know who I am –
and who I am

is not beholden to wankers,
I am not the servile vessel of flaccid stiffenings,

a pluck haired
pale mound

of flabby skin
shot through with a dark spot of keratin.

I'm only half-human,
it's not my best side . . .

DEAR BEETLE OF OUR LADY

Flesh covered concrete, that is what some people are.
Mimics who move – like you do.

Hold their hand out as if they know how to hold.
Attributes they loathe in themselves – they will swear, belong to you.

Impenetrable pebbles, painted, polished – eyeballs for stones.
It is your beauty they envy, the purity of particles in your soul,

the way you open that red cloak with such ease – as if you were born free,
your seven joys and seven sorrows are so perfectly spotted,

your instars have nothing at all to do with sneakers
and a certain (slightly) famous moth on the New York subway –

will not hand over their tears so easily, for they have learnt to fear you.
Clever layer of trophic eggs. Eater of aphids. Bringer of elation in summer
      meadows.

My darling Messiah! All I ask is that you close your elytra carefully –
      reflex bleed,
it's your luck they seek, vulnerability they wish to expose.

Whatever you land on is improved by your presence, this you will
      come to know
Dear Beetle of our Lady – you must count on yourself alone.

WORKSHOP, DAY ONE

It was the first
day

of engraving
bones

and the oracle
would not etch nice.

I had the dust
of an ancient ox forelock

on my skin
where the night before

your thumbs
had not been able to dig

far enough into sadness.
I had a box

to rattle with bones,
seven boxes actually,

I'd found thousands,
yellowing and forgotten,

neatly labelled
numbered in the attic.

I was informed
they were inferior bones,

which only made me
want them more.

I had a pot of gold for those bones,
scalpels, drills, knives,

sanders, paintbrushes,
poetry to engrave

under heat and blade,
the umber raw

reek of burning marrow
kept the workshop guys far away

until they complained,
the stench was felling them

they couldn't eat their lunch
or even really breathe –

I moved out to a courtyard
to burn bones in the snow.

ST MARY'S STREET

I'm wearing three French perfumes,
my heart is distracted,
the bar is too high.
Even in heels
I'm not so tall at all, not at all, and I didn't take the yellow pill but two
of the blue,
husbands honk their horns all night,
I don't sleep,
street men eat my bread.
Ten years ago I poured cinnamon on soup,
styled it out – it was not the first time we'd met,
the one before I can't remember,
I was busy,
don't ask me,
you were with another then,
still, we both knew,
this skin was smooth enough,
so how come you forgot instantly?
After so long,
this one's not on me –
it is down to you.

The first time you kissed me was in a bar
and the staff
were about to throw me out.
They were vexed
by my libations,
truly I could have gone another
round or ten,
not so . . . they thought,
fucking students, rank amateurs,
I was ready for the police
and a row of batons,
you took me by the hand
to an alley,
skin bare, exposed,
it was so cold, your coat –
was long, your tongue
flickered
across mine
like a candle,
my leg grazed up hard
against an ancient
wall, you gripped
my thigh
pulled me toward you,
I stood on tiptoe,
whispered in your ear – *fuck me*,
a spell so quiet . . .
you strained to hear it,
so low in tone and true in want
that you kept straining
to hear it,
alone in your bed

again and again,
even when I was far away
even when I was with somebody else
even when you were, too,
and you knew
science in no way negates
a true witch,
a true heart,
so, when I told you of the primordial
matriarch – thirteen point nine billion years old
who made everything . . .
in light and heat
and rage
all of destruction
all of desire
all of creation
the first source –
you said without slowing
in stride,
that's exactly
how I see you.

DIGITAL BONES

The thing is Betty,
with her digital bones,

has a bird
seeking butter

from her fridge, but more so
he wants to know

what she has hidden from him,
and I dare say

he won't find it
in the cooler.

The thing is, Betty's bird, who is seeking butter,
has a red beak,

wide eyes and big teeth,
but no hands to hold,

no feet to walk,
those legs – bend pretty well,

they go from table-to-door,
the thing is, Betty's boyfriend

can raise his voice
a tone,

it's quite funny
like a New Yawk Doll

but he's nameless,
his heart visible

only when he finally
sees butter on the table,

all yellow-gold,
just a mirage – then it's gone.

He could have watermelon.
There's beer in the fridge door.

Ham, tomatoes. In the end he is
hysterical and creaky.

Where is Betty?
Where is Betty?

Where *is* Betty?
That's the question.

Never mind the butter.
Where did his girlfriend go?

FIR TOM LEONARD

Dear Tom, d'ye ever hink
aboot how the streets in Spain urr dark

an there's a vicious cat posse at the entrance tae Kos,
unna light way doon

the alley
ay a back street

in Boulevard du 20 Aout

unna smell ay perfume
so sweet it's makin me shake ma fist at the ruins,

wummin plying their wares,
when they used tae just be girls too . . .

D'ye ever hink aboot the furthest part ay the desert in Egypt?
How there's ridges ay sand –

that huvnae seen hoof or foot or bike or tortoise or bucket or spade,
fuck's sake

they huvnae even seen
the shadow ay a plane

in seven million years!

The stars
are so bright on that spot . . .

ivviry night
they urr shinin!

D'ye ever hink . . .
aboot a lassie singing up a mountain

wi moonshine
brewin in the basement

an dugs at her feet
that look like fuckin wolves

an fireflies in jars,
and wooden spoons

in an auld tea tin.

D'ye ever hink
how much art ye'd steal fir her

if she smiled at ye
jist yince?

How ye'd kill the president stone dead
if she ivvir

asked ye tae
whilst laying in her bed.

D'ye ever hink how the ocean's currents are aw runnin?

Fishes swimmin
deep down in the darkest ay depths – right now

flashin electric,
blue an pink an green an huge fuckin eyes

racin out ay yir black abyss
teeth glintin as they slink and glide – on by.

D'ye hink aboot space?

How dark matter fucks us like eighty tae one and how death wish
comets are racin each other tae oblivion.

D'ye ever hink ay aw they dark restaurants – after hours?
Or, mannequins at four a.m. in Brooklyn Queens

by the Smokey Bacon Factory?

Or a nail bar in Peckham.
Or an art gallery just quiet as fuck when every cunt's finally gone!

An aw the wee dive bars wi two people drunk an holdin ontae each other
like everyhin is in their airms at that minute,

and quiet conversations
in poor neighbourhoods, an prisoners in right uncomfy beds

an guns held up steel an cold and metal
tae naked heids,

an hands pressed in prayer,
faces kissing earth

or tongues tracing the salt ay skin.
D'ye ever hink ay the elephants?

How thirr traipsing right across they plains
an how they buried

yin ay their ain an were slated
by a novelist

wi a bat attitude,
serious – bat as fuck she is,

an how it wiz kindae slanderous
how fast she'd drive

on the A1
past Fort Kinnaird

on a Monday at tits-up-a.m.
D'ye ever hink

aboot aw they bairns –
takin their virry first breath

whae
huvnae learnt yet

tae no trust the agents ay this earth –
D'ye ever hink

how we owe aw ay them . . .
so much mair

but how there's still a kindae
fuckin serious

as fuck
splendour

tae every minute ay aw ay this?

HOUSE WITH A PORCH OF FOUR SEASONS

One day I'm going to have a house with porches
on all four sides and views for hundreds of miles
so I can see black clouds keen towards the horizon . . .
a witch's sky to boil cauldrons of hate and desire.

One day I'll have two wolves who'll sit beside me
on that porch, they'll pace the ground knowing before
that an animal is trapped and needs release, and I will
be there with secateurs to cut through metal twine

with words to soothe and the warmth of my body.
I'll let that animal know – here, it does not need to be
scared in the night. When we bring it back to the lodge
of four views, to the sun and the moon, to the rain

and dawn, to the dragonfly and firefly, to the smell
of baking bread, heat – sweat, when hammering the roof down –
once again, to worn woollen throws on the sofa, that I kept
from when my boy was still a child. Our guest will rest until

they are well, then they will leave us in their own time.
One day – I'm going to have a room in that house
where the weary can stay and I can let them know
by the songs I still sing, I survived everything.

The kind of soul/heart/body – crimes people are not
meant to endure, let alone repeatedly throughout life
yet here I am – my hands are still open, there'd be porridge
in a pot in the morning, honey from a good friend's hive,

and countless books to line the many rooms of our minds.
All of that house will pulse – alive with love somehow,
in the grain of wood and creaks on the stair. Each room
will have a window to reflect season's change, bring

the coldness of the capitalist world – right down,
in volume, in regret and the wolves will patrol the porch
by my front door, day after day and I'll never need to talk
to them because they'll know what's in my head.

Regardless, I'll give them my voice, tell stories
of way back when and each month we will wait until
the fullest moon falls into the sky of our lives
to sit in a field out front with its one great – eye,

and we three will howl – the whole night long,
and sleep only at the break of morning, warmth on our skin
and hallways filled with the most golden light,
just as our dreams are – when the sun begins to rise.

EVEN WHEN YOU DON'T THINK YOU ARE

All summer it rained.
A white feather
fell onto a sodden pavement
on Madeira Street.

My morning coffee
wasn't strong enough to stop
me wanting
to drive to the island
at all moments.

There was a rainbow and thunder.
I got soaked.

When I came back, I sat in the window
thinking of me
telling you –
that I was like the mouse
you were talking about.

And how you paused
in that precise way
until I added –
nice and quiet –
I'm a wolf really though,
and you said,
damn right –
you are a wolf . . . .

And the undertone
of your voice
wedded
me solid
as any gold circle
to a path
many moons from now
where I will meet you
by clear waters
to seal
a soul contract
started many
lifetimes
ago.

It is true –
it has never been
just four days
or four nights,
instinctively
I drove –
hundreds of miles
but it was not our time.

WHO DID DUCHAMP?

Circumstances take the piss.
Blind Elsa returned

her review.
New York published poetry.

Girls with black lipstick
and cerise

face powder! –

Invisible spiders. Invisible. Spiders.

Attack the urinal.
Declare the urinal!

The urinal has an outlet.
Fully intact it is.

Confirm the urinal's lowly status!
The urinal is manufactured.

Identifying the urinal
is against obscenity laws –

it will lead
to imprisonment

so the legislators
say in razors.

The author does not describe
what it takes

to become a member
of society.

They intended to exhibit.
The urinal disappeared.

It was a convenient –
invisibility.

I wouldn't send tea balls
to the society

of independent
artists.

They can find their own urinal.

The urinal was disqualified –
it was not

submitted formally.
There are footsteps behind me

in the Duchamp
corridor,

knock, knock on a nearby door.
Don't look!

People being is so awkward.

Come on Queer Thing!
Where *is* my husband-wife?

Still wed to poetry.
All day it berates me.

Don't be mistaken,
I am many gendered,

well-versed
in almost-black lilies.

It's all about
the unadorned state of the inlet.

It was designed
for lead supply.

Eighteen inches.
Tip of the lip.

Triangle fixtures!
Fuck me, somebody.

Together there are no
facts to identify.

The private view was never scheduled.

I'm in factory-gate condition!
Leave her. Come to me.

If I played fair,
I'd be long dead –

I didn't ever need you,
do forgive me.

Flawed thing.
All want.

It was only a day after the rejection.
I played no part in it.

That judge fucking owes me!
Anyone else in here crazy lonely?

Touch me.
I'm against the distribution of fear.

Bad laws are no laws.

Such disgust and resentment.
Arouse me!

Therapist meets me once,
says I am highly

aroused, four times that hour.
He says – as a person!
What he means
is stark as winter.

He says I am all desire . . .
(the French kind)

with a capital D.

Extraordinary power.
You don't hold it.

It belongs to me.

This . . .
if I'm the mistress-piece,

then where
is my Victorian apartment?

You want to leave her
and come to me,

they all do lately –
it's tiring,

I'm having none of it.
I've faulty wiring.

Cosmic poverty . . .

I've none of that –
Still, they steal my beads.

Shitmutt!
That's all I have to say about you.

Nothing is forgiven!
Don't send hidden songs.

Poetry keeps attacking me.

We have become volatile.
These are our drinking years.

You and your throwaway gestures.
Fuck me.

I'm tired.
You are weak.

I am barely here.
I am bare. I am here.

Today I will fire all personal snipers.
I have no mother.

I know several artists.
They do not know me.

Arrest me.
I'm ornamental.

Fat and naked,
drinking breakfast brandy.

How I would have loved Elsa's
crestfallen canary.

One arm is celluloid.
The other is curtain rings.

He had no reputation.
The artists fled after he was exposed.

Idiots.
Most of them were not at all real.

I learnt to spit icicles.
I always was a god of war and female,

I have no choice in it.

Ejaculate.
Photograph me.

I'll fight you openly in the street.
Mannequin.

Said he wanted to piss on me.
But really, he wanted to kill me. Heat. Heat.

My grandfather would have murdered him twice
then brought him back to life

to lay at the back door
as a token gift for me.

This place is not a music hall.
It's a mental hospital.

I'm from here.
Love me.

Virile!
I've nights to spare.

Don't word me.
Be real.

I can't be curated.
I lied earlier.

I'm not paltry, or weak.

Nobody will stake me.
I'm ready made.

I'm a myth.
I'm heat.

I'm the air
on your skin,

whenever you ride
the London Underground

I am a lighthouse bride.
A cosmic agent.

Watch me sleep.

IT WAS AN EX-COUNCIL HOUSE ON THE SEA WALL, GRAFFITI ALL OVER IT.

At the second beach house
two herons
glide in every morning at low tide.

A round white sun-of-a-moon
spins her skirts,
as they stalk

a pebble shore in the haze.
My eye is drawn up from the lights
of fat red cargo boats

heavy with petrol
to skies
above me.

I sleep on the sofa
for months (in that dress)
with a baseball bat

beside me,
cos junkies flame-balled
my window

trying to create
a crack den with a view,
till I took over,

looked out each night,
like the lighthouse keeper
of eternal damnation.

Where a boat crashed
on my shore
at midnight,

its captain and skipper
slept on the beach
for four months

until they could get all the drugs
out, strip steel.
I'd glance down at their fires

at night,
sometimes take them candles,
or leave out pallets of wood

they'd drag past my door.
I'd stopped sending smoke signals
across to a summerless city.

I quit fiction, fabrication,
delusion and lie,
appealing as it may be for a poet and witch

to solely – see . . .
I am as much science
as I am seance.

I revoked my crazy
under the microscope
where it showed itself

only to be the clearest eye.
When kids set fire to the road nearby
I thought of Detroit,

Heidelberg's streets of art,
Tyree, Tyree, you'd have liked how pretty
I left that piss-stained

house, how immaculate
and bedecked
as it was by then in glass and white,

packing is the surest way
of arriving,
I no longer say goodbye.

I TOLD HER

I told her I was going to sleep
with every kind of woman
in the world,
in every country and she said – *that would take a long time.*

She wanted me to touch her,
but would not do the same for me.
She wasn't a starfish exactly, there were bits of me she wanted.
My darling pillow queen
was counting out – *the loneliest hours of her life.*

I didn't take her lack of investment personally.
I was having a thing with Bluebeard's wife,
and no woman should ever be
an expectation or, an ego transaction
leave that kind of – *shit to evil lawmakers.*

I told her not to die.
To stop taking mushrooms daily.
I told her that staying on the heavy pendulum
swing of a narcissist –
only ends in – *death after a long soul rape.*

I told her she should come to the beach house,
she could have the garage as a studio, it had a sea view,
its own key, it was not bloodstained,
I wouldn't talk to her if she didn't want me to.
She could – *recover from the trauma trap maybe.*

I told her she was beautiful,
talented, funny – that she had everything.
I'm not saying I didn't think about marrying her,
or happily ever being fucked over by life too much (both of us)
but she had a sickness for one who hurt her
repeatedly,
and I do get it, sadly.

I WAS TALKING TO WILL

There were dead pigeons
stacked in the operating room,

decomposing sheep heads,
half a frozen dog

in a cupboard somewhere.
Of course, a poet

is the right kind of person
to find it!

Nice shelves.
That's what the outcome was.

And how animators too
are a kind of poet.

Texture,
colour palette –

luminous
echo dissolve.

They play out love
in click frames.

Super eight,
whirr the puppets

this way
that way

the eye is watching –
don't blame me, Ghandi.

Eighteen hours
a day on paper.

Six months
for sixteen minutes.

Animatic purity,
compositing

chroma key, blue screen
a cat called Dom

and the making
of long bird

the blood,
the blood.

Dearest monkey love,
armature in stop frame,

digital bones
a skeleton with ball and socket joints,

19 bones in animation
compares to 206 in human

pare it down
who needs them all?

Those animations
have souls

all of their own.
There's a rocket in his eyes

have a heart,
it's fucking brilliant.

You know.
You know.

MARY DICK

I wiz born in White Horse Close
in *seventeen ninety-one*,

Two years later ma
brother (William)

followed,
a baby lost an two siblings left –

we played in oor yard in the Irish
area ay the Canongate,

it wiz a different district
(no Edinburgh then).

Oor days were punctuated
by the sound

ay a hammer
hittin horseshoes,

my Da wiz a farrier,
him an ma Ma

hud left a farm
in Aberdeen tae come

aw the way tae the city
tae raise a family.

At *four years* old we moved
tae Rose Street

unna a wee sister (Georgina)
joins oor fray,

there's three ay us then tae race
oot in the back lanes,

being telt tae watch oot
fir horses an carts ayeways.

Another brother joins,
the second James he is,

an in *ninety-nine* we flit tae Mud Island
(otherwise kent as Tumble Dust)

tap ay Leith Walk,
it wiz a wee bit ay

countryside or so it seemed!
We'd play on the grassy

slopes – next door's
(Mr Burt) wiz a vet,

the only yin in Edinburgh
so as weans we got tae see

aw the sick animals,
ivviry day fir *fourteen years!*

Ma brother William
an I watched

tae see exactly
what wiz done fir healing,

as carefully as we could.
In oor hoose another baby was born

but by then we'd lost three brothers
an a sister too wiz gone.

I wiz *ten* by then and struggled
tae shake ma sorrow

but Leith wiz frenetic.
Horses and carts

arrived endlessly
wi wood an stone

aw the way from the docks
tae the Top of Leith Walk,

building houses
an tenements aw year long,

the stables kept Da busy
an Mr Burt did his surgeries,

watched wi fascination
by ma brother an me.

We moved tae the North Side
then of Calton Hill

where Mr Wordsworth built
houses, horses and stables,

another boy was born (Samuel)
two years he stayed . . .

of oor great losses –
the Wordsworths understood,

of their nine born
there wiz only two left.

By the time I was *twenty*
William was working

wi Da as a farrier,
when a singer came tae town –

Elizabeth Feron,
her Da, Jean wiz a man

who'd tried tae start
a vet school in Edinburgh

aw the way back
when William wiz born,

then James Clark tried
again in the *seventeen nineties*

he wrote a book on it an died,
then in *eighteen eleven*

Alex Gray set off fir London
tae study at vet college

an I telt ma clever brother
it wiz time he did the same.

I washed an dried sheets
up on Calton Hill fir Ma,

kept house, learnt tae sew,
went tae market daily,

we had oatmeal porridge
fir breakfast, brose

or beef
an cabbage fir tea,

there wiz aye kale, or broth,
or fish, or flat bread,

cheese too an many,
many, many cups ay tea,

We moved tae Clyde Street
in *eighteen fifteen* –

so Da could set up
his ain farrier business,

put a forge in the courtyard.
I wiz offered tae read

some manuscripts,
unpublished as yet,

by Walter Scott –
I said; I think not,

I didnae agree
wi his political or religious

views, as fir his books
he went on tae write quite a few.

I wiz so excited
when ma brother

began tae study anatomy
wi the esteemed

Dr Barclay
at Surgeon Square,

yet yin glaiket chiel
called William

a common
working blacksmith,

tae which Doctor Barclay
replied, blacksmith

or whitesmith
he's the cleverest

chap here, I'll no lie,
that wiz much

tae ma delight.
Through Dr Barclay

ma Brother went
on tae study chemistry,

an begin the exceptional
practise of healing disease.

I wiz at William tae learn
as much as he could

tae teach me,
so mebbe I could help oot,

I telt Mrs Burt oor neighbour
ma Brother

wiz going tae be
a grand vet someday soon.

In *eighteen seventeen*
he took the coach

tae London,
tae study fir qualifications,

he wrote us letters,
we sent meal and tatties

transported by Leith smack
(fishing boat),

he put aw he learnt
fae his studies in one book.

I got on at him again –
tae learn how the college

wiz organised
down there,

tae work oot how it
could be done better,

he sat his exams
in *eighteen eighteen*

three months after starting
and he passed.

Soon as he got hame
aw we could do wiz talk

about how he could
start a vet school

tae take what he hud learnt
put it intae practise

and even mair important –
pass his knowledge on.

I'd long since made ma peace
that I wid nivvir marry

but ma Brother
fell in love

wi Sarah Wordsworth,
her Da wiz a banker

who forbid it,
the man thought

'we werenae good enough'
so she married

elsewhere
but her and ma brother

were close fir the rest
ay their lives

and he nivvir felt
for anyone

else the way
he did fir Sarah.

We lost oor last brother
John in *eighteen twenty-one*,

he wiz not strong,
grew lethargic then passed.

William would not
say his name,

again it wiz a most
painful loss.

I wiz doing the books
by then, fir Faither

an Brother, I wiznae intae
aw the fashion an elegance

and vanity ay parading
wummin on Princes Street,

I kept a keen ear oot though
fir what wiz gaun

on in ma city . . .
and much further afield.

William went tae France
tae study veterinary

practices there,
Da wiz made a Burgess

of Edinburgh,
ma books showed

we were making
good money, so eftir

much talking
they hired

Richard an Robert Dickson
tae design

an build
a proper veterinary school

wi accommodation
fir oor family,

it opened in *eighteen thirty-three*
ma Brother wiz just *forty*.

We moved intae oor
ain hame

for the virry
first time. Ma bedroom

wiz on the first floor
and I liked tae

keep ma window
firmly – shut.

Thomas Fraser
painted ma portrait,

an ma Brother
wiz such a great vet

his students learned
in the courtyard,

and I supported
William's idea

tae treat animals
ay the poor fir free.

I knew aw his students,
I made sure they kept

upright morals
or they would be delivered

before me
an they

didnae much like that,
they thought very well of me,

one named his daughter
Mary an many

became oor
lifelong friends.

In *eighteen forty* the students
wrote a letter

demanding the title
of Professor

be given tae ma brother,
that his school

became a college
and tae oor happiness –

they did.
Times hud been busy.

I stood up for
fellow Calvinists

in *eighteen thirty-eight*,
walked oot in support

at the Disruption
Assembly,

I treasured ma silver
disruption brooch

one of only
five hundred,

maBrother
refused tae support

a house tax
in Edinburgh,

tae raise money
fir the clergy,

he wiz prosecuted
in the small debt court,

I wiz an ardent
Liberal too,

a suffrage,
I still kept up on ma knowledge

of the issues
of the day,

especially
those that affected

the poor
or those in pain.

Oor house wiz full of visitors,
oor basement stocked

wi wine an spirits,
we built a place

by the sea
in Burntisland

an then in Aberdour
ma Brother

built a lot ay other
properties –

we'd sail over
tae Craigkennochie

by then we were
both in oor sixties,

I needed occasional
peace away

from business
an rhythms of the city.

In ma seventieth year,
we hud a photo taken,

staff an students
in the courtyard –

ma William had been made
vet tae Queen Victoria

so we carved
the Royal Crest

in stone tae show
his honour

off in the courtyard
but by *eighteen sixty-six*

ma brother William
wiz ill.

He hud been distressed
by cattle disease,

across the country,
he'd gained weight,

he could not breathe,
he hud pains in his chest,

he died on 4 April
eighteen sixty-six

of cardiovascular
failure, by then

I hud been a friend
to my beloved Brother

for seventy-three years,
his loss wiz terrible tae me,

I moved tae Craigkennochie,
people from Edinburgh

an beyond wrote
tae me in high esteem

fir ma Brother
I still hud his College tae run

and pass over
an it wiz a great difficulty

fir me tae have
in any way tae let it go,

knowing what oor family
and ma Brother

hud achieved.
A Mr Williams

hud taken it over for some time
but when he left

he set up a Vet College
in Gayfield house

which he tried tae call Royal –
I wiz not impressed.

I hud the council
put a stop tae that

an because of ma protests
that they preserve

ma Brother's
extraordinary legacy,

the council renamed it
The Dick Royal Veterinary College

in honour of his life
an what he did.

Only then could
I rest a wee bit more easy.

At ninety-two years old,
I asked Mr Young

(a Burntisland artist)
tae paint ma portrait,

then soon after I died,
it wiz *eighteen eighty three*

I made sure before I saw fit tae go
aw the property bought

an built
by our family

wiz given to the University of
Edinburgh, so it could

help other students
learn too,

so it could be of use
tae those in need,

an aw ma life
as a woman

I learnt a lot
aboot being a vet.

I studied an observed
in no small way

alongside
those men.

Fir aw those years
I hud knowledge

but I could
not practice,

however, I mentored
thousands so

at least they –
could an I made sure

tae preserve ma brother's
extraordinary legacy,

a life kept busy
is a life lived well.

I can say that I did aw
that an mair,

with a quiet – certainty.

MONKEY LOVE EXPERIMENT

This monkey is an orphan.
On the day of her birth she was separated
from velvet womb,
a voice ever-present turned to silence –
to say she has been adequately cared for since that day
is so far from the truth.

Her life hangs by a thread.
A monster holds her up to the moon.

A cloth mother is removed
from her cage.
Once a day, they observe her vital signs
deduce she would do anything to have her textile mother back again,
even if she was poisoned.

Harry Harlow deprived a monkey of all affection or attention
for the first eight months of her life.

When she was broken
he was curious
as to what she would do when given a mother to run to,
smugger than Satan he was – when she ran away.

If permanently deprived –
she could die from lack of love and utter loneliness.

Could anything be worse than this monkey love experiment?
You got it so wrong, Harry –
it wasn't that she could not love.
She didn't even know what a mother was you cruel fuck –
far less that she had a right to it.

It's a wire illusion.
It doesn't soothe me.

Monkey 105 I would have stolen you
from the depth of man's idiocy.
Every day I would have carried you pouch-to-pouch, gig-to-gig,
I'd have let you sleep on me,
your tiny hands wouldn't even have to hold on.
I'd not have let you go.

MORNING RITUALS

Getting dressed
in the morning

is a ritual
that begins

wan as a
Midwinter sun,

cars on cobbles,
bump-bump

like a minaret drum,
the body bends . . .

like a gnarled bough
on the willow

tiredness won't leave
on waking –

it just intensifies,
all day long.

I'm porcelain cold,
imperceptible in my sorrow,

shower steams the mirror
like a sigh,

still, got twenty-eight teeth
to shine,

hair reticent
to detangle,

a face to smooth
like each day

does not daunt
and nightmares don't walk.

Amber and ginger lily
sweeten my surrender

to another outside world affray,
front door opens

like a yawn,
go ahead now my girl,

turn the key –
these are the morning

rituals of me.

ONE DAY WE NOTICE THE WAY OUR PARTNER EATS AND ARE IRRITATED BEYOND ALL BELIEF

He measured me up.
My legs were ten mountains to climb.

Little arms
amused him and the smallness

of my hands
that had knocked down walls –

placed dragons
on daisy chain leads,

shined up their scales with ease,
how my feet were the size of a child's

and my toes made a mockery
of my mind.

He measured the curve
of my breasts – in want,

my nipple
with his tongue,

but one day –
he stopped measuring

not even my waist or laugh
or smile,

or each hair still warm
from the sun outside.

GOOD ART

Is the best kind of defibrillator,
I see your ventricles

and raise a soul
bound by flesh – yes,

marrow, blood and bone,
(it's in there the Élan vital

yet so often, to cut it out
needs an acuminous scalpel)

separate it from sinews
and muscle,

gristle,
tumour and fat,

the world is dying,
dearest darlings of the flesh hotels –

please gift it good art.

YOUR SEXTS ARE SHIT

James Joyce
only went & told Nora

a whole bunch
ay pish

to try & see her slit
up close.

Battery is dead, he said.

Trolls, don't know
positive fae negative, he said.

He said – her mad eyes
ensured a stranger fuck.

We have none of Nora's letters.
Only his word.

You should all take heed, he said.

Write dirty words
big! Coarse as possible,

and always – underline them.

PALE BLUE EYES

The more sorrow
I feel . . .
the bluer my eyes get.

It's the sea in there.

All those creatures,
in the lower levels, swimming
away, away –

to where the wild things dare not go.

THE DAILY DEATH

Every day you get up and you die.

It's a time.
Isn't it?

No knife required.

You are bloodless.
They never find your heartbeat.

It's too quiet.

Lit as you are like a Catherine Wheel.
You are every first love!

They say you haven't screamed for a long time.

Every three a.m. you shuffle out of bed.
Head to the bathroom.

You like to die with the light – off.

In the morning you brew the kind of coffee
that wakes corpses.

There is a locked cell, yes.

In there you shine away fear.
Can't last that though, that kind of glow.

A light like that?

It'd have you killed by morning.
Of course, it is, quite, as you say – habit forming.

Wake, die, wake, die. Wake. Die. Die. Wake.

PENROSE STAIRS

I am alone,
the space you vacate(d)

is cartoon like, it's
– Tom as he jumps

paws (and claws) out pronged
rips a silhouette

hymn – through a Technicolor wall
finally, we see the apocalypse

so clear
on the other side,

viewed by millions,
neatly silvered

is it not
in black and white?

You eradicated years
like comas –

instead of flowers
you sent flying moths

to eat my visions.
I had to be unseen

in my unseeing
were I to be a lie.

Ours was a death,
was it not?

Such dying.
Nothing else like it.

You took a soul tax
each time,

you'd raise the bill
by a thousand million,

rearrange the particles
of my intention,

endless confusion
could only be consoled

by the calm
of collection

in your arms.
It's been such a while.

Vampiric. Sadistic.
I may have soul

enough to spare
but your cupboards

drawn as I was to them
are – so tall and so bare,

we slammed doors
like prison wardens

on Penrose stairs,
you said you'd tell everyone

I'd been your lover
for years

if I died.
I thought it a bit of a clause,

most exes just fucked
with me whilst I was still alive.

You have no right to my
anything. Let alone eternity!

I never belonged to you
but the actions you took broke me.

It can't be taken back.
Not even after dust to dust.

I didn't deserve one minute of it.
A truth I'll always know.

Until I rest under the daffodils peaceful as a stone.

IT'S AFTER ALL OF US

So, breathe
whilst it is still in you
to do so
and leave
all your sins and sorrows
by
the door.

SOCIAL OUIJA

Every day I go online,
use the planchette

to divine
answers from the ether,

attempt tae conjure
up connection

or meaning –
I am looking fir a word,

a symbol,
reading between lines

of digital electrons,
beamed up intae space

and back down
intae a seance of electrons,

it's healing
I seek –

some feeling
ay connection,

tae another human
ma brain conned

tae reward chemically
fir likes or hits,

little lights
flicker in the dim

ignore the 3D world
fir the shimmer

ay a screen.
I scroll

wonder why
I keep coming here,

realise what I want
is those I've lost

to materialise –
I'm looking

fir my closest friends
whose funerals

I attended,
an who I miss

mair than they
will ivver know

yet a part
of my irrational

brain –
keeps scanning

the crowd
the web

the clouds
the street

anywhere
in fact at all

hoping,
hoping,

tae meet their eyes –
again.

WHEN THE REPTILES CAME

When the reptiles came, we were bow arrowed.
When the reptiles came, we were part-woman – part-gun.

When the reptiles came, we held hands as they approached.

When the reptiles came, we stood in love.
When the reptiles came, we did not trade in our dreams.

When the reptiles came, we did not lower our eyes.

When the reptiles came, we rose above them.
When the reptiles came, we fought to expose their lies.

The reptiles thought they could use our empathy against us.

Use it as a weakness over which they could take hold.
They manipulated every bit of decency.

Sought only to annihilate our souls.

When the reptiles came, we met them in the hallways.
When the reptiles came, we blocked all the stairs.

When the reptiles came, we watched them from the windows.

We let them think it was still in us – to care.
When the reptiles came, we loaded up our weapons.

When the reptiles came, we did not give in.

When the reptiles came, we sang to all the children.
When the reptiles came, we took them unawares.

THE AUSTRALIAN

I used to like to smoke
whilst you went down on me,
exhale,
blow a smoke ring,
drag it deep,
you liked me in red shoes,
black nails,
occasional latex.
You wrote me menus in biro to select what I might like to eat,
worried
I never took enough,
tried to make me go with you to the video store
but the vast expanse
of grass
had blades all made of glass
and when you left
to go back to your own country
I didn't lock the door,
cos it was broken
but I did have a hammer under my pillow
and a million
places yet to live.

THE DEATH OF COMPLIMENTS

And one day every woman
has to ask herself

if she is willing
to be loved

by an
ordinary man,

hang up her Saturn rings,
let go stars

caught in her hook
bodice

and Mercury
womb,

not scare him,
with the shock of her nearness

he'll have to place that
further away

up on a shelf,
a shadow one step behind

where before –
glitter in her soul

drove him mad
with love.

Soon
she will have

to ask – or cajole,
or incite . . .

it will be the death
of compliments.

Such
a stage . . .

he will tell her
he has heard her stories

and yes, he has seen
her shine

thus begins
her decline

unseen –
an iris decays,

in all the chores
of no-thanks,

she begins to wait
on the moment

he might see
her again.

Is it better
to walk from this,

remain
the person she was

before he had to
make her less of what she is . . . . ?

Which is not ordinary
or even close,

truth is,
he can only really

see her
when she is – not his,

age old
and not without consequence

is joyless
rapture.

We die
in tiny moments

un-
seen

abandonment
takes

all roads,
demands what was once unique

no longer gleam so loud,
that it becomes, ordinary.

THE DEVIL

You kept me like I slept in a box
and you could put the light on or off.
I didn't ask for the lies – nor the chaos,
you always did like me best tied up in knots.

You know it's true.
The Devil got to me – and he came through you.

THE EXPECTATIONS OF OTHERS

That I should smile.
And.
Be patient.

Corset my unfamiliar
so it won't
bomb too many institutions.

My presence
is too pure
and relentless.

Silly, silly, silly.
To think what you wanted
was really me.

Well – I won't revoke
my expectations
of being cherished.

Just as I am.
Just like this.
Sin-fucking-cerely.

THE PIVOT

Cludge like I am since your mind-wind caught me, upstream
radioactive a peptide storm of no escape

in one way or another.
It's been dark a lot where I have turned,

at best I should never have been your lover, wavering,
I have chosen not to turn to you

now pain is a line spearing soul from spine
to heart, it won't ease – I loved him like he was a part of me,

a pivot sadistic as delusion,
truth left so many notes and I ignored them.

Reality – must give us a sense of who we are
when we are not endlessly wondering,

pincer-woven, stab-webbed,
all the jibes and more of the worst

to save life and sanity – no less.
Keep breathing child, and – walk.

TIM HECKER

Plays bass at an exact frequency
to vibrate
through atoms.
Electrons
travel through spinal cords as light,
brains seek
to be atomized.
I'm distracted watching a young man with one arm
on a date
and he is cute,
so is she,
and their table is round.
I am ready
for it to hit again,
lower the frequency,
audio spectrum – scatter glitter in my veins.
Synapses
spill
where there used to only be dissection
in this room.
Horses present and dead and anatomically correct,
veterinary surgeons
training
outside it was the olden days –
where now there is only a solid sub bass presence.
It has
a brilliance,
does this vibration and somewhere on stage in the dark
a human heart
radiates.

TATTOOED MAN

I read you – with fingers
and tongue,

talked so quiet
in your ear you weren't sure if it was my soul

inside your mind,
and we were both hurting someone.

I picked you up in a car
at a train station.

I'd never met you before
but I knew your silhouette

from some other time.
Your eyes on me in the dark,

my voice, your reply,
winding roads with no lights.

We climbed the rocks,
so I could show you my favourite sea.

It was a witch's sky.
Waves crashing.

You told me how you held pain in high value
and of the hurricanes –

when you were a child,
how you'd ignore all weather

warnings and drive instead
to the edge

of the world,
walk down to the shore,

when big waves began to roll in,
you'd wait – tempest

wild, feral
with longing,

for the hurricane.
You wouldn't ever leave

because it's where you
belonged, the place was in you,

if it was to be torn apart
you'd be right there –

arms wide open
to welcome those winds.

It was a thing, wasn't it?
That belonging.

SO

I can't remember your smell anymore.

I look for signs.

Pigs pogo.

When is the exact right stage to blood-let what is too deep in our veins?

We talk in our minds every day.

I see the cloth mother, but I can't tell you.

I want you like a crack pipe.

Pain riddles my bones.

Songs don't soothe.

When I cry, and cry and crying has its own cry too.

Search every crowd for one pair of eyes.

We become a memory.

Silence cloaks me.

Stars are rising.

You are deadly.

You are still gone daily.

I open the door and my heart is in a box, but it is not addressed to me.

I don't breathe for three months.

I am a casket and a cigar and a child and a pervert and an outcast queen.

Underworld me.

I am not yet liberated.

I am the most alone I have ever been.

Pick up a dagger.

Spell-cast.

You are annoyingly ubiquitous.

All seas pound hard as they can – on every shore.

You turn up in dreams.

I can't make you go.

I think of us in front of the fire.

Drugs can't touch it.

I stride to all places in shit-kickers.
I'm so weak I can't get up.
I lay in the hall like a dead spider.
It took me twenty-five years to admit how much I wanted you.
I walked away rather than risk your loss.
When will I stop walking?
It's far too late in this life (or the next) – to tell you.
You are gone.
Autumn falls in summer.
I rearrange furniture.
On every single chair you are irritatingly smiling.
I ask real nice – leave my fucking mind alone.
I refuse your imprint.
I no longer allow the hostage situation (in regards) to my soul.
An exorcism is ordered.
I am voodoo.

When I touch myself I never think, about you.

A NOTE ON THE AUTHOR

JENNI FAGAN is a poet, novelist and screenwriter, she has twice been nominated for the Pushcart Prize. Jenni was selected as one of Granta's Best Young British Novelists after the publication of her debut novel, *The Panopticon*, which was shortlisted for the Desmond Elliott Prize and the James Tait Black Prize. Her adaptation of *The Panopticon* was staged by the National Theatre of Scotland to great acclaim. *The Sunlight Pilgrims*, her second novel, was shortlisted for the Royal Society of Literature Encore Award and the Saltire Fiction Book of the Year Award, and saw her win Scottish Author of the Year at the *Herald* Culture Awards. Her most recent novel, *Luckenbooth*, was shortlisted for the Gordon Burn Prize. She lives in Edinburgh with her son.